A FEARSOME
FORCE OF NATURE

My Amazing Life in
Drama, Education and More:

A FEARSOME
FORCE OF NATURE

My Amazing Life in
Drama, Education and More:

A Memoir by Flonnie Anderson

ISBN: 978-1-61846-053-0

library partners press

a digital publishing imprint

330 ZSR Library, Wake Forest University, 27109

"A FEARSOME FORCE OF NATURE"

"My Amazing Life in Drama, Education and More"

Credits:

Front cover photograph courtesy of The Little Theatre of Winston-Salem

Back cover photograph by Bob Brower

Illustrations by Michelle Richardson

Printed in the United States of America

First Edition, First Printing, 2019

Table of Contents

DEDICATION

I DEDICATE THIS MEMOIR TO MY ANCESTORS, my parents, my husband, my siblings, my offspring, my students, my community and all others who have meant so much to me during the wonderful journey of my life.

The task of jolting my memory was entrusted to Ken Keuffel. He prodded me gently to recall incidents long forgotten. He has been thorough and persistent, unlocking so much cherished past. Thanks, Ken.

A very hard task for me has been selecting -- from among the many letters, essays, short stories and poems about me a few which I think validate my identity. My final selections represent my guiding vision and passion.

Again, thanks to all who have encouraged my nurturing spirit. You have made each of my golden days a celebration.

INTRODUCTION

I LIKEN MY LIFE IN THE THEATER TO AN EPIC, unusual play. Epic because I'm in my 80s, and the theater still keeps me busy in one way or another. Unusual because the "play" consists of numerous acts--each of which gives me a different starring role.

I act on stage and screen. I do voice-over and commercial work. I write material for solo shows and for plays and musicals that thespians in my native Winston-Salem perform. I direct numerous stage productions featuring either companies I establish or students I teach at several high schools. Many of my high school students want to continue acting into early adulthood, so I establish a company for them to do that. While I emerge as something of an entrepreneur in black theater in the 1950s and '60s--organizing troupes for kids at recreation centers and, later, founding the first black community theater in the South--I never forget that the arts should also bring different peoples together. I play an instrumental role in integrating Winston-Salem's community theater scene, both as an actor and as a director. I become the director and part of a multiracial cast that performs on a mobile stage that brings theater to neighborhoods all over Winston-Salem during the 1970s, helping ease racial tensions in the process.

I teach drama and other subjects in high schools in Winston-Salem and elsewhere for 33 years, favoring methods that often deviate from the traditional. Thankfully, these methods achieve the desired results--which is what my bosses care about, not the fact that I sometimes raise eyebrows among colleagues or even stir up controversy among policymakers who are made uncomfortable by a play's content (something that art is supposed to do from time to time, right?).

I believe that everyone in my classes or ensembles has talent; that it is my job to bring this talent out and put it to best use in a show; and that anything is possible for my students, be it performing in the nation's capital or in a debate competition traditionally reserved for whites.

In some instances, I find that recruiting a cast works just as well--and has just as much educational value--as choosing one from among students who join drama clubs on their own. Several of my students become professional actors, and one of them even appears in a high school production of a classic play before becoming a star defensive end in college football and the pros.

I retire from teaching in 1989, eliminating my involvement in high school theater. But don't think that the curtain has fallen on the final act of my play. As you'll see, when the right project comes along, I can and will participate. My son, Rudy Anderson Jr., doesn't call me "a fearsome force of nature" for nothing.

ACT I

Beginnings

M Y PASSION FOR DRAMA, particularly as it relates to performance and education, has its roots in a safe, happy childhood that revolved around a loving family, the church (which offered families all manner of activities) and school.

I was born in 1930 and grew up at 1609 Clark Avenue in Winston-Salem, NC, the first child of Henry and Janie Thomas. During my early childhood, my two sisters, Lena and Jeannette, and I never saw the screens that ensnare the children of today with one video game after another. We rarely stopped engaging in play of our making--which, arguably, is the basis for improvisation skills that actors develop in conservatory programs.

In 1934, I was 4, Lena was 3, and Jeannette was 2. I once wrote down my recollections of that time: "We play all day long--in the house, on the front porch, in the front yard, in the back yard, from sun up to sundown." We also had plenty to play with, including dolls and tricycles. We'd climb a peach tree, jump rope or play hopscotch.

My upbringing confined me to the black neighborhoods of a segregated Winston-Salem--but nothing about that situation stood in the way of my ambitions. My mother made sure of that, stressing that education was my ticket to a successful life. She herself was a dedicated educator, leaving by bus early each Monday morning for a week of teaching grades K-8 in the one-room all-black Sandy Level School in Mount Airy. When she returned home each Friday evening, her excited, adoring children were always there to greet her. While Janie was away, either our father, who worked the midnight shift at the Hanes Knitting Mill, or our Aunt Genoa, who lived next door, cared for us.

I attended my mom's Mount Airy school for a year, in 1935, after which I opted to attend schools in Winston-Salem. I still have vivid memories of a long bus ride to Mount Airy, followed by a 10-mile walk to a one-room schoolhouse heated by big chunks of wood that had been thrown into a pot-bellied stove. I remember that during the winter of my year in Mount Airy, a long and

2

sparkling icicle often hung from the mouth of a pump by the school that provided the students water. And a resident who lived near the school introduced me to pigs for the first time.

Among other things, my mother taught me and the other children at Sandy Level to recite poetry and prose eloquently-- passing down a family tradition that amounted to my first lesson in drama. Sandy Level, being a classic one-room schoolhouse, enabled me to soak up the full sweep of the curriculum offered to children through grade 8; Sandy Level kick-started levels of academic attainment that resulted in my testing out of and skipping at least two grades in elementary school.

The result: I graduated from Atkins High School and began my freshman year of college when I was all of 15 years old. This kind of thing was the norm among "gifted" children at the time, and looking back I must say that I enjoyed the challenge of mastering more advanced work. Had I not skipped grades I would almost certainly have been quite bored and, quite possibly, a behavior problem.

By the time I had entered Atkins High School (at age 11), I was developing into a well-rounded child. I sang in school choruses and productions of operettas, and I'd do readings for my English teachers. I also excelled in basketball, about which I became so passionate that I pursued little else outside the classroom, unless asked.

During my youth, the seeds of my interest in drama were sown by mother. She loved the poems of the late Langston Hughes and other black poets so much that she learned many of them by heart and recited them in public. She recited black poetry at least once a month during special programs at churches, becoming a favorite guest artist for many a Winston-Salem congregation in the process. I was often in attendance at my mother's recitations, soaking up the words and the captivating way she delivered them.

My mother's recitations of poetry showed me what the best Shakespearean actors know: Great words, no matter how obscure their meanings may seem to silent readers of the printed page, come to life with a dramatic clarity that most any audience can grasp when they are read out loud in masterful fashion. So back in the 1980s, during the early days of the Stevens Center, the principal performance venue of the NC School of the Arts (now the UNC School of the Arts), I would always think of my mother's excellently performed recitations for inspiration when I read literature of my choosing during the center's "Shorts for Lunch" series.

Incidentally, the audience for "Shorts" presentations consisted overwhelmingly of whites who must have wondered what accounted for my fascinating, thespian-friendly upbringing among blacks. Little did they know, as my husband has pointed out, that so many of the Thomases were great actors--even if they didn't know it!

Anyway, looking back on my childhood, I now see how much my mother's recitations inspired my chosen career paths in drama, which included directing, acting, and teaching. These career paths crystallized following my decision to major in drama at West Virginia State College then (now West Virginia State University), a historically black school in Institute, West Virginia. I earned a bachelor's degree in theater arts. I had originally intended to major in English and French at West Virginia State, along with earning a teaching certificate. At least that's what I told my mother, who discovered that I had changed my major--and still needed a certificate--on the day I received my degree.

I still remember vividly what happened after commencement. My mother called me "fool" etc. because I lacked a teaching certificate (an imperative for many working women in 1949, because teaching was one of the few professions open to them). She also reacted coolly to a drama teacher who approached us and suggested that I join him and other students on a trip to California, where they would participate in an acting program.

For me, drama eventually came to hold greater appeal at West Virginia State than French or English. French and English kept me confined to the classroom. With drama, though, there were exponentially more possibilities, and most were outside the classroom. Yes, a drama major studied plays as literature and wrote papers about them and other aspects of the theater. But a drama major also could perform on stage or work behind the scenes, building sets, for example, or designing costumes or directing. I played the leading role in a West Virginia State production of *Antigone,* for example.

ACT II

The Entrepreneur Emerges

DURING MY COLLEGE DAYS, I began to realize that there was a downside to my mother's recitations and other theatrical presentations frequented by the blacks of Winston-Salem. Usually, they were confined to a school or church setting. I felt that theater in my community should enjoy a broader stage. Therefore, in the summer of 1949, shortly after I graduated from college and returned to Winston-Salem, I set about creating one.

The first step in that process took hold when the city's Recreation & Parks Department appointed me summertime leader of teenagers at the city's recreation centers. I was also in Winston-Salem for two other reasons: to court Rudy Anderson Sr., my future husband, and to get my teaching certificate from North Carolina Agricultural and Technical State University in nearby Greensboro. After earning my teaching certificate, I taught for a few years in Georgia and South Carolina, gaining some teaching experience before returning to Winston-Salem, where my first teaching job was at Atkins High School, beginning in 1958.

Recreation centers functioned like summer camps during the time that I worked at them. Parents would drop their kids off at centers on their way to work with the expectation that they would participate in all manner of activities, from baseball to knitting. I felt that drama needed to be in the mix of offerings at rec centers as well. When I approached Lloyd B. Hathaway, the city's recreation director about starting a drama program, he strongly supported my idea.

Encouraged, I soon organized drama groups in each of several recreation centers that served the black community of Winston-Salem. We presented shows at the centers and in several other venues--mainly at Wentz Memorial United Church of Christ, but also at Salem Academy, Paisley Senior High School and Winston-Salem State University. I also organized festivals at which each of my drama groups presented plays as part of a competition.

The kids were glad they could get in front of people and perform, having been made to feel confident on stage. Thankfully, too, video games were not competing for the attention of kids back in the 1950s! Our community, which felt unwelcome at predominantly white venues, became excited about theater and began looking forward to productions.

Looking back, I can point to several explanations for my success at getting youth theater off the ground at the recreation centers. For starters, nobody had done what I was doing before in Winston-Salem's black community, so my programs had a novelty appeal, particularly among people who were looking to broaden their cultural horizons. Parents became interested in what I was doing; they encouraged their children to participate.

I found early on that a gradualist approach worked well with the kids. Rather than announcing the production of a play and holding auditions for it, for example, I handed out scripts of a play and asked the children to simply read various parts. In time, I might ask: "Do you think you could memorize these parts and act out a scene?" The kids would embrace the challenge, do a little more each day and before you knew it, we were working on a full-blown production.

Often, I wrote the script, lyrics and music for shows. I also became known for programming plays that called for very large casts. This ensured that just about anyone who wanted to could appear in our shows, and it had the effect of attracting big crowds of patrons, many new to theater, who wanted to see their family members and friends act on stage.

I made sure that drama was a fun activity by orchestrating games and improvisation exercises that soon attracted the interest of more and more kids. The improvs the kids did were particularly effective at stimulating their imaginations; each would rest on a different scenario from everyday life.

One of my key teaching philosophies began to crystallize as I led the youth drama troupes at the rec centers: Young people are very creative and imaginative, and they have lots of great "material" in them. You can draw this material out and more if you inspire them to open up and go wild. Nothing they come up with is ever wrong because we always make something big out of their ideas.

INTERLUDE

It's Time to Thank the Family

BEFORE I CONTINUE RECOUNTING MY AMAZING LIFE in drama, I'd like to thank my mother and my husband for their support of my career, beginning when my husband and I started a family in 1952. I now see I led a charmed life, always being able to count on a family member to play the role of surrogate parent when a theater project took me away from family for a time.

My parents, Henry and Janie Thomas, supported me in different ways. Henry told me repeatedly that he'd transform our backyard barn into a performance venue for my theater company.

As for my mother, she emerged as a visionary, establishing one of the state's first licensed kindergarten nurseries, where I often dropped off my children on the way to work. I say "visionary" because she started her day-care center in the 1950s, well before the feminist movement would lead to a widespread demand by working mothers for day care.

My children loved my mother's day-care center, which became a part of a community of family and neighbors who looked out for them as they walked to school or to visit my mother in her nearby home. It was not uncommon for a neighbor to call me when, for example, one of my children decided that rolling around in snow was far more fun than continuing a journey to their grandmother's house. Today, I can scarcely believe that we enjoyed this kind of lifestyle.

It's also worth noting that my husband and children often participated in my theater projects, either as actors or as stagehands. (My son, Rudy Anderson Jr., appeared in his first Flonnie Anderson-directed show when he was five years old!) All my children acted well, having inherited that talent from me, and all of them sang well, just as their father does.

This family buy-in amounted to the best kind of support for my career, and often it enabled me to look after my children while on the job.

ACT III

A Community Theater
for Blacks Is Formed

MY INTEREST IN CREATING COMMUNITY THEATER for blacks in Winston-Salem extended to adults as well. So, in the first couple of years following my graduation from West Virginia State, I began organizing casts and stagehands for productions I directed. Shows, including *Antigone*, took place at recreation centers, Wentz Memorial United Church of Christ and the college that became Winston-Salem State University.

These early efforts went so well that the people involved in them began pushing for the establishment of a community theater that would afford my projects the fundraising, public relations and other benefits of a more formal organization run by a board.

The theater guild's early participants included the late Dr. Joseph N. Patterson and Mrs. Daisy Chambers. Chambers, who acted and choreographed for my shows, enjoyed a long career as a teacher and administrator in Winston-Salem's public schools.

Dr. Patterson wore several hats. He played the piano well enough to serve as a music director for musicals I directed. He served as Wentz Memorial's pastor beginning in 1948, and he was a beloved professor of education and philosophy at Winston-Salem State College. Dr. Patterson would prove very helpful to me in securing venues for shows at Wentz Memorial and Winston-Salem State.

In 1951, the Community Players Guild, the first black community theater in the South,[1] was established. In time, we had everything that any community theater needs to succeed: storage space for costumes and props; a permanent venue for rehearsing and performing; a clear mission in terms of programming; a pool of enthusiastic actors and stagehands eager to participate as volunteers in show after show; and a loyal audience.

---

[1] Our claim of being the first black community theater in the South rests on the fact that when supporters of the Community Players Guild researched the constitutions etc. of other community theaters for blacks, they could find none in our region.

The venue for rehearsing and performing emerged after Lloyd Hathaway, the director of the city's Recreation & Parks Department, worked with the Winston-Salem school system to secure the auditorium in the then-new Paisley Senior High School for that purpose. Recreation & Parks also gave us a room for storing props and costumes.

The moment was right for the guild. As I suggested earlier, theater for blacks in Winston-Salem was confined to the occasional production in a church or school setting, so opportunities for black amateur actors were extremely limited. The guild rectified that situation overnight, not only for actors but also for techs and others who worked in support of them behind the scenes.

From the start, we had lots of fun. But we also aimed to showcase production values that were every bit as good as those in a professional production. I took rehearsals seriously and expected my casts to do the same. This meant, first off, that cast members were to arrive around 30 minutes before the official start time of a rehearsal to do those exercises that would ready body, mind and voice for optimal performance.

Once rehearsals started, I could be demanding. I became known for saying things like, "Honey, you know you can do it better than that. Let's give it more effort."

Chambers and I recently reminisced about my directing. She said: "You were a professional. You always strived for excellence." Chambers also said that she came to think of rehearsals as a kind of on-the-job training that taught you most everything that an acting student might learn in college.

Larry Womble, who later became a prominent member of the North Carolina General Assembly, also acted in several guild shows. When we talked recently, he remembered long rehearsals that didn't seem long.

"It was something I wanted to do," he said.

The guild went strong for a good 15 years, even when family/maternity obligations and out-of-state teaching jobs took me away from it for short periods of time. My three children-- Rudy Jr., Mica and Luron--were born between August of 1952 and November of 1955. I also taught briefly at high schools in Damascus, GA (1953-1954) and in Beaufort, SC (1957). In 1958, I returned to Winston-Salem for good, having accepted an appointment to teach English and run the drama club at Atkins High School.

Each guild season had something to suit every taste. We staged a serious play in the fall, a comedy in the winter and a musical in the spring. And because I favored shows that called for large casts, the chances for landing a part were pretty good for most anyone who wanted one. I also wrote new parts into established plays, albeit for actors with considerable potential only.

The shows staged by the guild made for a rich, highly anticipated season of performances each year. They ranged from *Witness for the Prosecution* to *South Pacific*. The latter, incidentally, featured a chorus drawn from the Twin City Choristers, of which my husband Rudy was a founding member. It also reflected my strong belief that blacks should be given every opportunity to appear in *all* shows--even those that were not originally conceived as vehicles for predominantly black casts. And if the casting of a black in a particular role clashed with someone's idea of authenticity or historical accuracy, so what?

Theater is about life. We all experience life and we all breathe the same air. So, in most cases, race should not dictate who plays which parts in any show. Talent should. So, give a talented actor a chance to succeed in a portrayal of any role, no matter the color of his/her skin. I tried to exemplify this ideal when I gave parts to whites in several guild shows.

The only exceptions I made to the aforementioned casting policy emerged when *clarity*, not believability, was on the line. For example, in Lorraine Hansberry's *A Raisin in the Sun*, which I have staged several times, the Youngers, a black family from Chicago's

17

South Side, come into enough insurance money to move into a bigger dwelling in an all-white neighborhood. Mr. Lindner, a white man who represents his neighborhood's home improvement association, pays a call on the Youngers shortly before they're to move into their new home. Instead of welcoming them, however, he tries to give them money so they will stay out of his neighborhood. In my productions of *Raisin*, Lindner has either been a white or a lighter-skinned black so that there's no confusion about the racial prejudice at the heart of his encounter with the Youngers.

Is the theater of today more likely to embrace the Everyman concept of casting I began championing decades ago? Certainly, several signs point in that direction, representing progress that would have seemed unimaginable 20 or 30 years ago.

In the summer of 2015, for example, when much of this memoir was being written, *The New York Times Magazine* ran a story about Taye Diggs (*When Stella Got Her Groove Back*) playing the title role in a Broadway production of *Hedwig and the Angry Inch*.

"Is this not madness?" wrote James Hannaham, the profile's author. "Black America's most eligible bachelor is about to play a glammed-out Teutonic genderqueer mash-up of Nico and Axl Rose?"

Diggs had dreamed of portraying Hedwig for some time. "But I didn't think it would ever happen," Hannaham quoted Diggs as saying. "I assumed that nobody would ever have the open-mindedness to cast this character black."

And then there is Mia Katigbak, the co-founder and artistic producing director of the National Asian American Theater Company. Katigbak has "made it her mission to send Asian-American actors wherever the theatrical canon may lead, "from 'Our Town' to 'Othello' to 'Antigone,'" Alexis Soloski wrote in *The New York Times* on June 25, 2015.

In July of 2015, Katigbak's company--aiming, in Soloski's words, to "drive home the versatility of Asian-American actors and their ability to represent the American experience" -- began presenting Clifford Odets' *Awake and Sing!* at the Public Theater in New York. The play, from 1935, chronicles three generations of a Jewish family living in a Bronx tenement.

Scene from Lorraine's Hansberry's "A Raisin in the Sun"

INTERLUDE

Recreation & Parks

RECREATION & PARKS HAS COME UP SEVERAL TIMES in my memoir. And for good reason: the department was always very supportive of my work in establishing theater troupes for kids and adults, and for that, I will always be thankful. In time, Recreation & Parks even made a show-mobile available for transporting my theater troupes and me to recreation centers and other venues with the goal of reaching as many patrons as possible.

The show-mobile presentations, which usually entailed performances of plays I'd written, were part of an effort to perform in as many different parts of Winston-Salem as possible, easing racial tensions in the process. They began happening in the 1970s as part of Urban Arts, an arts council-supported program designed to make the arts more inclusive of blacks. They rested on the idea, which I strongly supported, that it was far more effective to take the show to underserved populations than to try to lure such audiences to more established, less welcoming venues frequented by whites.

ACT IV

Winston-Salem's Community Theater Scene Is Integrated

As I INDICATED IN THE INTRODUCTION OF MY MEMOIRS, I played an instrumental role in integrating Winston-Salem's community theater scene, both as an actor and as a director.

In 1956, for example, I became the first black to act in a Little Theatre of Winston-Salem production, playing Tituba, the voodoo-chanting slave girl, in Arthur Miller's *The Crucible*. This was significant:

Winston-Salem was rigidly segregated at the time, and blacks just didn't figure in theatrical presentations patronized by whites. When Little Theatre shows of the 1950s and earlier featured black characters, they were played by whites in blackface--a practice that's offensive to blacks because whites in blackface mocked blacks with portrayals of demeaning stereotypes.

Doris Pardington, who became the Little Theatre's first manager-director in 1950, was determined to bring this racist state of affairs in her company to an end, albeit quietly. I say quietly because it was only in 1989 when she first spoke publicly about her motivations for my *Crucible* appearance. This was in a "Tarheel Sketch" profile of me that ran in the *Winston-Salem Journal* when I retired.

"I knew what I wanted, and I didn't want to put any more blackface on white actors on the Little Theatre stage," she told the *Journal*'s Genie Carr.

A little background: When I began staging guild shows, I invited Pardington to attend them. She did, and we developed cordial relations as theater colleagues. She also became acquainted with my work in acting, because for some guild shows, I not only directed but also performed, playing, for example, Bloody Mary in *South Pacific*. These dynamics contributed to a tacit understanding that Pardington would cast me in *Crucible*--if the powers behind the scenes approved. These powers were the board members of the Little Theatre and the Arts Council of Winston-Salem and Forsyth County, and I soon learned that Pardington had to work especially hard to win them over. When they "finally gave in to Pardington, we were close friends from that moment on," I'm quoted as saying in a program commemorating the Little Theatre's 2004-2005 season, its 70th. I also learned recently that Mrs. Gloria Diggs, a Winston-Salem arts enthusiast, has acknowledged recommending me for the part of Tituba.

Georgia West has been a Little Theatre volunteer since 1965. When she worked with Pardington, it was mainly as a makeup artist. Although West wasn't around for *Crucible*, she's not surprised that Pardington succeeded in casting me.

"When (Pardington) spoke, you moved," West said. "She was the leader. You were the follower."

My appearance in *Crucible* happened at a time when many whites in Winston-Salem engaged in ugly, even violent protests against integration anywhere. And yet, the Little Theatre's collective focus remained not on my breaking the company's color line but on *Crucible*, both during rehearsals and performances. This was as it should have been.

Crucible, from 1953, is an important play in any era. But its dramatization of the witchcraft trials in Salem, Mass. was particularly meaningful in the 1950s, becoming an allegory for the McCarthyism that persecuted so many at that time. I could and did put my acting talents on full display with my portrayal of Tituba, winning over Pardington and many a Little Theatre patron in the process. And Beverly Wolter, in her review of the production for the *Winston-Salem Journal*, wrote that I "turned in an outstanding piece of work as Tituba, caster of spells and caller of Satan." (Wolter also wrote for the *Twin City Sentinel*, which was closed in 1985.)

The rest of the *Crucible* cast accepted me and we went about our business in a cordial manner. My husband Rudy and I accepted invitations to cast parties. West isn't surprised to learn all this, noting that theater has a long tradition of "taking people where they are," regardless of race or sexual orientation.

The Little Theatre's *Crucible* had a business-as-usual feel to it, and I credit this to some clever maneuvering by Pardington behind the scenes. For example, as Carr reported in 1989, Pardington persuaded Winston-Salem's newspapers to recognize me as a "character actor" playing Tituba, not "a Negro." Wolter's review bears this out, identifying me as "a first-time Little Theatre actress" only.

To the best of my knowledge, reports that I became the first black to act for the Little Theatre appeared in two publications: *Jet* magazine, which had a national audience, and a newspaper aimed at a black readership outside of Winston-Salem.

Both West and Chambers suggested recently that I was the right person to begin integrating the casts of Little Theatre shows. They praised my professionalism, noting that I arrived at each rehearsal prepared, got along well with everyone and produced high-quality work.

My success in *Crucible* had at least three positive effects. First, when I walked around town after the production's run had ended, people complimented me on my work in the show. This made me feel very proud and boosted my confidence that I could take on similar projects.

Second, my appearance in a Little Theatre show led to even more efforts to integrate community theater in Winston-Salem. In 1957, Pardington began asking me to recommend guild actors for her shows and I began casting Little Theatre actors in guild shows. A few years after that, blacks began auditioning for Little Theatre shows on their own.

Third--and most important for me--my personal involvement in Little Theatre shows was just the beginning:

In April of 1959, I was cast as the Neighbor woman in Tennessee Williams' *A Streetcar Named Desire*. Reviewing the show, Wolter wrote: "In a large cast, there was not a performer who played his part poorly."

Another article even reported on the audience's reactions to the opening-night performance. Several patrons, including James Hart and Mr. and Mrs. Ralph Hanes, doubted that the amateurs in our cast could do *Streetcar* justice. (They had seen the original New York production of the play, which opened about 12 years earlier.)

After they saw *Streetcar* in Winston-Salem, both Hart and the Haneses were astonished at how well we had performed. Hart was quoted as saying that he "enjoyed (our production) thoroughly." Mrs. Hanes called the production "superb, just superb."

In 1969, I was cast as Catherine in a Little Theatre production of Truman Capote's *The Grass Harp*. The play revolves around four people who leave their homes to live in a tree house because they feel oppressed by relatives and neighbors, according to a summary Wolter provided in her review.

Wolter found the production a mixed bag. She wrote that it "had many laughs, well-intended ones, meant to couch (its) message in light, easy-going ways." She praised an elaborate set that included a tree house. But in her judgment, the actors "often were wooden and hesitant" and sometimes sounded "as if they were still doing a line rehearsal with books."

Wolter wrote that Flonnie Anderson "established a distinct characterization at the outset and maintained it." My portrayal also impressed the Little Theatre, which awarded me a Golden Award for best performance in a supporting role.

The crowning moment in my involvement with the Little Theatre happened in 1972, when I became the first black to direct a show for that company. This was *Cactus Flower*, a two-act comedy by Abe Burrows. In the play, which originally ran for 1,234 performances in New York during the 1960s, "a man's young girlfriend demands to meet the wife who is keeping them from getting married — a wife that the man invented to keep the girlfriend from getting too close. He asks his spinsterish assistant to pretend to be the wife, which leads to complications," reads a www.playbillvault.com summary.

Looking back, I recall vividly how I felt during the *Cactus Flower* gig. I felt proud to be directing a multiracial cast for a major theater company in Winston-Salem, my hometown. I felt excited to be helping actors to improve their skills. And I felt a liking for the show because there were some New York City accents and idioms in it that I hadn't encountered as a director before. I always liked the challenge of taking on something new.

The Little Theatre's *Cactus Flower* did very well at the box office, becoming the most financially successful nonmusical show in the Little Theatre's history up to that time. Most performances sold out, and there was a waiting list for the production's last two weekend performances. An additional show on a Thursday evening was added to the production's run to help satisfy demand.

I attribute our success to several factors. A talented cast, chosen from a large turnout at tryouts, did a great job with Burrows' strong farce material. I had an established reputation for doing very good work among many blacks, and a large number of them bought tickets to the see the show. The Little Theatre's fans became quite curious about *Cactus Flower*, having never been to a show directed by a black person.

Most important, I had no qualms about my directing abilities, having had numerous opportunities to develop them with the guild and with students I taught, and I felt good about the training I had received at West Virginia State College.

Roger Richardson, a white brother, played Igor Sullivan in the *Cactus Flower* show I directed. He recalled recently that he had appeared in just a few other shows before joining our cast. He said

I was "perfect" for community theater because I knew how to work with the range of talent and experience at the heart of every community theater's cast of amateurs. "You were warm and friendly," he said. "You were on our side, trying to get the best work from us."

I approached *Cactus Flower* with typical Flonnie Anderson resolve. I looked it dead in the eye, expressed what I wanted to do and did it. And what, specifically, did I do?

First off, I made no assumptions about knowledge levels among the amateur cast members I was directing. I made sure that everyone understood, for example, what I meant by such terms as "upstage" and "downstage."

I introduced my cast to vocal exercises that would help them project clearly. I taught them movement exercises that would calm them down (if they were hyper coming into rehearsals) or that would motivate them. This drove home an important point: Success on the stage depends on quality preparation of individuals off the stage. I expected my actors to learn their lines three weeks before opening night; it's very hard to get better at each rehearsal if you're constantly struggling to remember lines.

I circulated a complete rehearsal schedule with the expectation that an actor should start doing preparation exercises

30 minutes before his/her call time. They were all the on the same page; in other words, they all knew what they had to do.

I was a stickler, causing some interesting dynamics to emerge during rehearsals. For example, I sometimes needed to correct some of the technical deficiencies in the speech of some of my Caucasian brothers. When that happened, they'd look at me and, feigning horror, say, "How dare you tell us how to speak!" We'd all break up laughing, but as rehearsals progressed, they did try to get their tongues right so they would speak the language the way I wanted them to speak it.

At the end of the day, *Cactus Flower* was the kind of positive experience that inspired its cast members to participate further in community theater. "Some of us kept together" for subsequent projects, Richardson said.

I ran into Richardson recently during a trip downtown. It had been a long time since we'd last seen each other. But it didn't feel that way.

"I still feel close to you," he said. "It's like nothing's happened in between."

.

ACT V

At the Same Time as Some of Her Little Theatre Activity, "Mrs. A" Takes Her A-Game to Atkins, Directs a Special Antigone

I NEVER FELT THE SLIGHTEST BIT SHY about recruiting anyone into the casts of the shows I directed at schools. Just ask Carl Eller, a Winston-Salem native who attended Atkins High School, where I ran the drama club in addition to teaching English from 1958 to 1960.

Eller was among the best defensive ends in the history of college football and then in the National Football League. After a stint at the University of Minnesota, he was from 1964 to 1979 one of the legendary "Purple People Eaters," the famed defensive unit of the Minnesota Vikings. He has been a member of the Pro Football Hall of Fame since 2004.

In the fall of 1959, Eller's senior year at Atkins, rehearsals for a drama club production of *Antigone* began, and had yet to cast a King Creon. I began looking about the hallways of Atkins and concluded that Eller would fit the bill. He was big and imposing, and he had a deep, resonant voice befitting of royalty.

When I approached Eller with my idea, he seemed flattered and willing. There was just one problem, which Eller pointed out: Football practices took place at the same time as rehearsals.

"That's OK," I remember telling him. "I'll talk to your coaches."

Eller's coaches knew and respected what I was doing with drama in our community. Although they heard me out, they couldn't quite believe what I was requesting of them. They resisted. I persisted. In time, we came to a compromise. I could have Eller whenever practices had ended or he was no longer needed at them.

Thankfully, King Creon doesn't appear in every scene of *Antigone*. So I was able to rearrange rehearsals to accommodate

Eller's football obligations. Still, there was just a small window of opportunity for Eller to practice his parts. I remember that he arrived at rehearsals while he was still in his practice uniform!

I'm not privy to how this all went down among Eller's teammates in the locker room. He may have gotten some good-natured ribbing for his thespian activities. Or some of his teammates may have gotten a bit jealous and sought to appear on stage as well; three of his teammates were cast as guards after Eller joined the production.

In the end, of course, all that matters was how Eller and the rest of the cast performed. They acquitted themselves admirably in a production that also featured appearances by Larry Womble and my son, Rudy Jr., who played the page that accompanied King Creon wherever he went on stage. Rudy was just five years old.

Eller made quite an impression, memorably expressing his fury at Antigone over her intention to bury Polynices, her brother. The burial, which would be in defiance of Creon's orders, prompts Creon to order that Antigone and Ismene, her sister, be put to death.

My casting of Eller illustrates the importance I placed on the artistic development of young black men under my supervision. I always felt that they would be better citizens, husbands and employees if they came to view school as more than preparation for a job and/or a way to advance in athletics.

INTERLUDE

Frenetic, Fruitful Fun of the 1960s

IN JULY OF 1961, MY DAUGHTER DEIRDRE WAS BORN, becoming my fourth bundle-of-joy. I had been granted maternity leave from Atkins High School to care for her. I envisioned becoming a stay-at-home mom for at least the next three years.

But in early August of 1961, I was summoned to a meeting with Superintendent James Adams at the Central School Office. He told me that Andrew B. Reynolds had been named principal of the then-new Anderson Senior High School, and as a reward for accepting the appointment, could hire six teachers of his choosing. I was one of Reynolds' selections. Might I return to work in September?

I was flattered--but conflicted. Teaching had become an integral part of my life, and the offer to teach at Anderson might not come again. At the same time, I kept thinking that I could not leave Deirdre.

My mother persuaded me that Deirdre would be well taken care of at her day-care center, just as my three sons had been when they were younger. During the year that Deirdre was born, Rudy Jr. would turn 10, Roscoe Mica 8 and Raymond Luron 7, so I felt that my sons could help look after Deirdre as well.

I went to work at Anderson and stayed for 10 years, teaching classes in English, speech, drama, the humanities and publications.

Before Deirdre's birth, my sons had done what many energetic, fun-loving boys do. They climbed trees in nearby woods, played with crickets in a nearby pond and went on romps through our neighborhood. (We were living at 315 W. 25th Street at the time.) They went to father-son banquets at the YMCA, attended summer camps and vacation Bible schools and often saw movies at the Lincoln and Lafayette theaters, which catered to blacks. They sometimes got into fights at home, breaking lamps and end tables or leaving large holes in hollow doors.

After Deirdre was born, my sons still played a lot. But they would turn a lot of attention to their baby sister. For example, they and a couple of students kept a watchful eye on her while I supervised after-school activities at Anderson. The activities included rehearsals for school plays, talent shows, drama competitions and speech festivals. I was also involved with the school's newspaper and yearbook, and I attended my boys' football games.

Deirdre grew up in a household that rocked. She became swept up in the whirlwind lives of her siblings and parents, lives that would embrace both the arts and athletics. I did my best to stimulate my children's' interest in the arts, taking them to symphony concerts, quality movies and other cultural affairs. I introduced them to the North Carolina High School Drama Festival of Plays, and I encouraged them to become proficient writers and adept orators. As you'll see in a subsequent section of this memoir, Rudy Jr. wrote *Take Me Higher*, a play that I staged in the 1969-1970 school year at Anderson; the production was well received by students, parents, faculty and administrators. After that, Rudy attended Hampton Institute, an historically black university in Hampton, Va. (In 1984, the school changed its name to Hampton University.)

My sons had fun with music. Rudy Jr. played the saxophone, and his brothers each played a brass instrument. Our living room became the site of community band practices. The boys also sang in school choruses and appeared in operettas.

Rudy Sr. became president of the PTA while all his sons attended Kimberley Park Elementary School. The boys had to do their homework each day after dinner whether they ended up at our home or at their grandmother's.

When my sons became teenagers, they participated in several extracurricular activities, making my husband and me very proud. Rudy Jr. played the alto saxophone in The Superiors, a popular band later renamed Opus 7. Roscoe Mica became a trumpeter for the Moravian Easter Sunrise services. And Raymond Luron became the first black emcee for the "Spring Follies" show at Reynolds High School.

Each of my sons played varsity football at a different high school in Winston-Salem. Rudy Jr. earned all-city and all-state honors in football at Anderson; Roscoe Mica played for Parkland and Raymond Luron played for Reynolds.

As for Deirdre, she would do particularly well in athletics, becoming a star basketball player at Carver Junior High School and eventually lettering in three sports at East Forsyth Senior High. She was all-city and all-state in basketball at East Forsyth, and she was a dynamite softball player, not only at East Forsyth but also in a community recreation softball league, which awarded her several trophies.

There were some down times--as when, for example, President John F. Kennedy and Martin Luther King were assassinated in the early 1960s. Roscoe Mica recalls that his grandmother's grief became uncontrollable when she heard the news one morning of Kennedy's death on the radio. Also devastating was the news of a football player losing a leg because of a football injury.

But on the whole, life was very good to the Andersons during the 1960s. As Judge Denise Hartsfield quipped during one of many speeches she made at our church, Wentz Memorial United Church of Christ: "I sure would like to have grown up in the Anderson household. They had fun, y'all."

Flonnie Anderson

ACT VI

We Are the Champions

I ALWAYS THOUGHT THAT SPEAKING the English language with eloquence was just as important as reading with understanding and writing proficiently. There were two reasons for this. First, I found much beauty in the sound of English language; I expected my high school students to capture that beauty in the way they spoke it. Second, I felt that black students who enunciated English words with clarity would counter negative stereotypes about the quality of their speech.

So, in early 1969, when I learned that Wake Forest University was hosting the 13th annual North Carolina High School Speech Festival, I wanted the students in my humanities course at Anderson High School to participate. (I had been teaching at

Anderson since the fall of 1961.) Robert Brower, the principal of Anderson at the time, gave me the green light to apply and provided bus transportation.

Our appearance at the festival would mark the first time that an all-black school had competed in what had been an all-white event that drew hundreds of students from 30 high schools in the Southeast. Naturally, I wondered how this would affect my students. Brower, though unfailingly supportive of me, worried that our participation in the festival might be a tad too bold, that a poor showing might hurt my "stature" among Anderson's other teachers. My colleagues often asked, "What's she doing now?" when I did something outside the norm, and Brower picked up on that.

I said nothing to my students about the festival's racial makeup until a week before the festival's start date, opting instead to make sure they worked hard on their preparation. Practice sessions, which took place after school and on the weekends, were intense. At one of the last practice sessions, I said: "All I want you to do is step on that campus and show them that you know what you're doing. You might find that you're the only black school there."

During the festival, students vied for superior ratings in the following categories: acting of scenes, oral interpretation, extemporaneous speaking, after-dinner speaking, original oratory and radio announcing. Schools competed for the highest overall score in speech, which was based on scores in the categories.

The festival lasted two days. Early on, it became obvious that my students' preparation had put them in a position to be quite competitive. My son, Rudy Jr., did particularly well. He garnered superior ratings in after-dinner speaking, radio announcing and acting. He and Wayne Ledbetter, one of his Anderson classmates, both received a superior award for original oratory.

Best of all, Anderson High School achieved the highest overall score at the festival. All the Andersons--"Mrs. A"; her son Rudy; and several other Anderson students--had done themselves proud.

Flonnie Anderson

INTERLUDE

My Children Excel in Theater

AS TIME PASSED IN THE 1970S AND BEYOND, my children would land leading roles in several productions I staged for the Flonnie Anderson Theatrical Association (FATA), which evolved from the Community Players Guild.

Raymond Luron became known throughout the community for his rousing portrayal of Purlie the Preacher in the musical *Purlie*. "Winston-Salem's Purlie sure is handsome and he can sing too," one patron noted.

Rudy Jr. and Roscoe Mica were lauded for their show-stopping portrayals of Zeus and Nickles respectively in Archibald MacLeish's *J.B.: A Play in Verse,* a dramatization of the Job story.

Deirdre was noted for the intrigue she created as Medea in the Sophocles' tragedy of the same name.

Rudy Jr., Roscoe Mica and Deirdre starred in *Remus,* the musical I adapted from *Tales of Uncle Remus.* Deirdre played Stacy, the student who gets lost while on a field trip with her class and teacher. She encounters some of the animals that her class has just met as they study the Remus tales. Rudy Jr. and Roscoe Mica played Br'er Rabbit and John Q. Fox respectively.

We lost Raymond Luron after a brief illness in 1991--but not before he made his mark in show business. In the movie, *Mr. Destiny* (1990), he plays the umpire who yells "strike three" in the beginning and end of the movie. In the film, an "unhappy Larry Burrows (James Belushi) sees what his life could've been like had he made that winning home run as a teenager." *Mr. Destiny* is still being screened around the world.

Raymond Luron also wowed Livingstone College with his singing group Unique Isolation during the four years he was a student at the school. He also served as the group's choreographer.

Raymond Luron, along with Roscoe Mica and Deirdre, also sang in Plush, a group that became quite popular in Winston-Salem. They performed at the old Atkins High School, in Fries Auditorium at Winston-Salem State University and at the Stevens Center.

Deirdre appeared in *Loose Cannons*, which was filmed in Wilmington, N.C. And everyone in our family, save Rudy Sr., appeared in the film *The 5th Quarter* (2011).

Flonnie Anderson

ACT VII

Controversy Erupts

IN THE 1969-1970 SCHOOL YEAR, MY SON RUDY Anderson Jr., a senior in my humanities class at Anderson High School, wrote a play called *Take Me Higher*. The play mixes candor about real problems with hope that they can be overcome. While it dramatizes the notion that such vices as promiscuity, hate and the erosion of the family are chipping away at America's foundations, it suggests that a reversal of these vices can heal America's ills.

Or as a written introduction to the play put it, *Take Me Higher* "examines several areas of contemporary belief on which America trembles. The attack on these beliefs is so severe that the America of today, caught between these devastating forces, trembles and decays. But she is replaced by another America. This America offers hope."

I arranged for *Take Me Higher* to be staged in Anderson's auditorium as part of a special class project. The performance was very well received, not only by Anderson's students and faculty but also by parents and various administrators of the Winston-Salem/Forsyth County Schools. It would be presented that summer at St. Andrews Presbyterian College, with similar success.

For me, *Take Me Higher* came to exemplify the creative potential of high school students--so much so that I felt an encore presentation was in order. During the following school year, when desegregation of the county's schools led to my being transferred from Anderson to Parkland High School, I began rehearsals for a staging of *Take Me Higher* at Parkland as well, casting everyone in my 35-member drama class. I did so in the belief that *Take Me Higher* would not only be a great learning tool for the student thespians but would also help break down racial barriers among them; the class was half white and half black.

The students certainly furthered their knowledge of drama and they achieved unity--but not in the way that anyone expected.

They presented three performances of *Take Me Higher* at Parkland during one school day in November of 1970. Students and faculty attended these presentations, as did parents and friends of cast members.

In *Take Me Higher*, certain characters embody (and are named) such words as Love, Hate, Sex, Patriotism, Religion and Hostility. In several instances, the play's lines include poetry of Sir John Suckling or others who were writing poetry when the play was written. So several lines in *Take Me Higher* amount to fairly lengthy monologues.

During one of the Parkland performances, though, Religion's monologue turned into a kind of impromptu dialogue--with the Rev. David Jones, the pastor of what was then Bible Moravian Church. Jones, who'd been sitting in the audience, stood up and started ranting about what he perceived to be the inappropriateness of the production.

I hadn't anticipated this reaction, nor had the students in the show. Instead of becoming flustered, however, Wallace Wright, the student playing Religion, adapted brilliantly. He used pauses in Jones' rant to "respond" with different lines in the script. The exchanges came off so believably as "dialogue" that the audience felt they were a part of the show. Wright followed a rule I demanded of all my actors: No matter what happens in the audience, you play it.

Though Jones and Wright really did have something going in dramatic terms, I was horrified. From my seat in the back of the auditorium, I began signaling frantically to several male teachers. Once I got their attention, it was all I could do to persuade them that the pastor was not a part of the production and that he should be removed from the auditorium immediately. After what seemed like an eternity, the teachers hurried down the aisles, grabbed Jones and ushered him out of the auditorium.

Several copies of the *Take Me Higher* script were in circulation during rehearsals, and it's possible that one of them ended up on Jones' desk. But to this day, I'm not certain how Jones found out about *Take Me Higher,* much less why he felt moved to protest against it in the highly disruptive way that he did. While the performance he interrupted continued without incident, the controversy surrounding his actions was just beginning.

The controversy is both a short story and a long one.

The short story: Jones had some powerful allies, namely two members of the Winston-Salem/Forsyth County Board of Education. They echoed Jones' objections to *Take Me Higher* with such vehemence that future performances of the play were banned by Marvin Ward, the superintendent of schools. (At least one such performance had been planned on another school day at Parkland before the incident with Jones.) Newspapers quoted one school board member as saying the play was "ridiculous and completely absurd" and "sacrilegious and unpatriotic."

My drama students continued working on *Take Me Higher* even as its future became shrouded in doubt. In January 1971, a five-person review committee of the school administration saw a private performance of *Take Me Higher.* After taking into account questionnaires answered by people of various school groups who also saw the private performance, the committee deemed the play suitable for senior high school and adult audiences. Shortly thereafter, the school board upheld this judgment by a vote of 4-2.

It's worth noting that the school board had not wanted to take a stand on the play unless another performance had been planned, hoping that the controversy would fade away quietly. It only did so when supporters and opponents of the play forced the issue during a public-input section of a board meeting. The supporters, which included teachers and parents, felt that a decision upholding the review board's judgment would "discourage continued controversy and adverse interference" in academic affairs, according to media accounts.

In March of 1971, the Parkland thespians under my supervision presented *Take Me Higher* at the North Carolina High School Drama Festival in Raleigh, where it received a superior rating. I have never been prouder of my students, who pressed on despite the controversy, and I am still proud of *Take Me Higher*'s author for the work he did.

As for the long story of *Take Me Higher*, this took on the feel of a seemingly endless soap opera masquerading as a forgettable morality play. It still leaves me scratching my head all these many years later. It is documented in a scrapbook I compiled throughout the controversy. This contains my personal notes, some correspondence and more than 70 articles, editorials and letters to the editor.

Let's begin with one board member's position. This came under extraordinary scrutiny and prompted considerable public debate. More than half of Parkland's 1,600-plus students signed a petition rebuking him. And in a scathing letter published in *Hitching Post*, Parkland's newspaper, senior Richard Whicker chastised him for "statements (that) constitute a hasty generalization and pre-judgement which is alarming by a person in your position." He demanded that the board member "retract the hasty and derogatory remarks which you have made concerning Parkland's play." And he called on him to "reaffirm our faith in a school board that can be approached and affected by the sentiment of its students." The letter was signed by 337 students, aka Parkland Mustangs.

The board member responded to Whicker's letter with one of his own, writing that "language which declares on the stage of a high school that we should disregard the advice of our elders about sex, that God was created by man...or that fibers of our flag will be stomped into the ground, is pretty tough language." He also wrote that "when we put such language on a school stage, whether to illustrate a point or not, we dignify the very preachments and tactics of those forces which are trying very hard to destroy us and, which we all agree, we seek to defeat."

At that point, word of the *Take Me Higher* controversy had spread well beyond Parkland's walls. Editorialists and writers of letters to the editor began voicing their views in the *Winston-Salem Journal* and the *Twin City Sentinel*.

A *Twin City Sentinel* editorial essentially weighed in on the exchange of letters, concluding that the negative philosophy of the school board member expressed in his letter "will not win out in the long run."

"Because if it does, it will then become necessary to censor the Bible (starting with II Samuel 13, Genesis 39:7 and most of the Song of Solomon); to black out *The Mod Squad* and many other TV programs that portray a world that is not exactly perfect; and to suppress almost any other work of fiction or drama which assumes that intelligent men and women must know something about society's evils and dangers before they can cope with them."

As if to underscore divided opinion on the school board, the editorial also quoted another member of the school board: "When the play began, I at first thought that here was something which wouldn't be taken right. But after I saw the whole play the characterizations evolved into things which were bad with society and showed that there was still hope for America. It just distresses me that so much furor has been caused, because the end of the play showed that good wins."

Essentially, the letters to the editor either supported the *Sentinel's* position or the opposing position. Nobody seemed to take a middle-ground view.

At the end of the day, the controversy surrounding *Take Me Higher* raised some serious questions: Are academic and artistic freedoms inviolate all of the time, particularly for students nearing the maturity of adults able to make their own judgments, or just some of the time? Should a school play be censored by policy makers merely because they're offended by its contents and/or wish to placate constituents with similar views? Or should they view it as free speech deserving of a fair and complete hearing?

These questions will undoubtedly inspire differing answers, and while I respect all of them, I'm still astonished that Jones, and other supporters either a) protested material they had willfully taken out of context or b) took issue with material whose ultimate aims they misunderstood. I'm also astonished at a letter Jones sent me in January 1971. In it, the pastor contemplates "the threatening judgment suspended over your soul."

"Your soul is too precious to Jesus to be sentenced to flames of eternal hell," he wrote. "Will you then repent openly and please go on to produce a play entitled *Take Me to Heaven*?"

I'll not dignify such drivel with a response. But I will expose Jones' baser motives for interrupting *Take Me Higher*. The play's staging at Parkland took place against a backdrop of massive racial desegregation in Forsyth County's public schools. This change, like all changes, caused considerable discomfort for all involved. But I was determined to make it work, as were many of my colleagues. Jones and his supporters were not. To them, *Take Me Higher* had become a monster directed by a black teacher who advocated sexual activity among youth, flag burning and hate for the country. They hated the idea of a mixed cast, believing that it brought black and white students too close together or even

59

enabled a black cast member to say nasty words to a white one. Jones was so infuriated that he burned *Take Me Higher*'s script in front of a local cameraman who recorded this unfortunate event on a WXII news program for all to see.

If Jones was trying to sabotage desegregation, he failed miserably. Indeed, the ruckus he and his supporters caused only deepened the solidarity that Parkland's community showed in its response to the controversy the play had caused. With few exceptions, we all came to love each other, to hold dear the best values illustrated in the play. Our bonds became so tight that the negative forces could not win.

My first year at Parkland could have been a very tense one for me, but it turned out to be one of my best. The school's principals, teachers, students and parents came to respect my talent and expertise, contributing greatly to my calm. *Take Me Higher* set the stage for many years of even greater success for Parkland's drama program. In time so many students wanted to take drama classes that we could not accommodate them all.

INTERLUDE

The Humanities at Parkland

URING THE 1970-1971 SCHOOL YEAR, as the *Take Me Higher* furor was raging at Parkland Senior High School and beyond, I also began teaching a class on the humanities. This course, open to seniors only, explored how the principles of literature, music, architecture, dance, painting and sculpture influenced our view of life. (I had taught a similar humanities course for three years at Anderson Senior High School.) The students in my humanities course at Parkland expanded their knowledge by attending movies, local symphony concerts, plays and art exhibits.

Each of three groups of students participated in a creative project involving a sonnet: In the first group, each student composed a sonnet. In the second group, each student set a sonnet to music. And in the third group, each student illustrated the meaning of a sonnet, using an arts discipline of their choice.

Deborah Horn, who later became a principal in the Winston-Salem/Forsyth County Schools, took the humanities course I taught at Parkland. When asked by a reporter of the *Winston-Salem Journal* to describe her experiences in the class, she said:

"We learned that to appreciate art, one must experience it. It helps us to think deeper than we did before."

INTERLUDE

Some Thoughts on Parkland's Teachers and Race

SOME WHITE TEACHERS AT PARKLAND simply did not have the skills to discipline their classes. They did not know how to interact with black students and their parents. I believe they really wanted to -- but nothing in their education had taught them anything about marginalized children and how they learn. Many concluded early on that these students were slow and did not want to learn. They had this pity thing going on, having decided early on to do little to develop the abilities of these students.

The few white teachers who resisted desegregation took things a step further with black students, deciding not to teach them at all even as they drew paychecks. Their mode of operating became: So long as a black student was not disruptive, he could spend his days in the back of the class, not involve himself at all in learning and still pass a course. If he became disruptive, he would spend his days in the discipline room.

I had already worked with one white teacher, Mr. Frank Ruark, the American history teacher at Anderson, who took a different approach. The black students under his supervision soared. Even black athletes did well under Mr. Ruark, having been encouraged also by their coaches. I wished that he could have followed me to Parkland.

I decided that no negative "stuff" would mar my teaching skills, no matter where I taught. By this time, I had concluded that my skills would be valuable in most school settings.

ACT VIII

The Parkland Players Excel at Parkland and Beyond

IN MARCH OF 1971, the Parkland Players, exceptionally fine student thespians under my supervision, made their debut at the North Carolina High School Drama Festival in Raleigh, where they received a superior rating for their production of *Take Me Higher*. The troupe would distinguish itself not only at future festivals but also in several non-competition performances outside of Winston-Salem.

Some of the Parkland Players contributed to non-Parkland productions I staged. Some created original works that the

Flonnie Anderson Theatrical Association would showcase. And some would go on to land professional jobs in acting or related disciplines.

Festivals My scrapbooks are full of citations for the players' excellent work at festivals. In 1974, for example, the Carolina Dramatic Association, an outreach group associated with UNC Chapel Hill, awarded the Parkland Players a Distinguished Achievement in Play Production award for a production of *The Great American Goof: A Ballet Play*, which was selected from a catalogue of plays published by The Dramatic Publishing Co. The association also awarded the Parkland Players an Excellent Achievement Award in play production for *This Property is Condemned*.

In 1972, the North Carolina High School Drama Association presented Parkland with two Critics Distinguished Awards. One was for "overall Production and Effectiveness in stage presentation of *Foursome*, the other for "overall Production and Effectiveness in stage presentation" of *The Death of Happy*.

In late April of 1977, the Parkland Players represented the southeastern states in the American Theatre Conference Festival in Chicago, having won a state competition at Duke University and then the Southeastern Theatre Conference, a regional competition held March 1977 in Norfolk, Va. At the Southeastern conference, the Parkland Players practiced the techniques of meditation concentration that they learned in drama classes to calm down. All of these shows were one-act plays selected from Dramatic Publishing catalogues.

The Parkland Players did particularly well at the Southeastern Theater Conference. They received several honors for best play: a certificate of merit awarded by the judges; the N.C. State trophy; and the Southeastern Theater Conference grand trophy. They also received $500 from the American Scenic Design Corporation. Debbie Latham '77, a senior member of the Parkland Players, was named the conference's best actress.

The best play in question was *Back to Creation*, which I wrote with James Weldon Johnson's poem "The Creation" in mind. The *Winston-Salem Journal* quoted me as describing it as "a show in mime, movement and narration depicting the creation of man, his development from childhood to adulthood, his subsequent move away from his spiritual center and his final recognition of the importance of his relationship with God." I recreated the show for a special program at Wentz UCC.

The Parkland Players Become Professionals Latham's honor at the Southeastern Theatre Conference entitled her to participate in a 10-week apprenticeship in drama at Hartford, Conn. She worked with professionals during her apprenticeship and received a salary. Later, Latham acted professionally; for example, she played Mary Urmond in the annual outdoor production of *Blackbeard: Knight of the Black Flag* in Bath, N.C. But in time, she developed a passion for costuming and became the wardrobe chief for several movie moguls.

Latham wasn't the only Parkland Player to make it as a professional. Jihmi Kennedy '75 became known for his roles in several movies, including *Gung-Ho* and *The Rosemary Murders*. He is most revered for his portrayal of Sharts, a former South Carolina slave who becomes a Union Army sharpshooter, in the movie *Glory*, which stars Denzel Washington.

Latham and Kennedy's success recalls that of Fay Hauser-Price, whom I taught at Anderson. Hauser-Price has several movie and television credits, in addition to her work as a producer and director. She played Carrie Barden in *Roots: The Next Generations*, the CBS mini-series from 1979 that is based on *Roots: The Saga of an American Family*, Alex Haley's celebrated novel. She also landed parts in *Good Times* and in *The Young and the Restless*.

Performing Outside Winston-Salem Our success at festivals was beginning to be known beyond high school drama circles.

In the fall of 1975, just weeks before America would begin celebrating its Bicentennial in 1976, a play by Dr. Elizabeth Welch came to my attention. Welch, a professor emerita at Salem College who had taught American history there, had sought unsuccessfully to find the right director for a production of her play, *That Banner in the Sky*. An acquaintance of hers recommended me; in time, she requested that I direct the Parkland Players in a performance of *Banner* as part of a winter gathering of the American Association of University Women (AAUW) at Salem College.

Banner tells the story of this nation's heritage through its greatest symbol, the American flag. The production would be part of a "creativity" theme AAUW was exploring. The AAUW, which was founded in 1881, sponsors several programs aimed at improving the lives of millions of women and their families.

I was flattered by Dr. Welch's request that I direct her play, and I was quite impressed with her script, which she wrote in 1945 in response to her growing alarm over the "way people mumbled and ignored the pledge of allegiance to the flag," Bill East wrote in the *Twin City Sentinel*. The play is a choric drama, which Welch described as a cross between a play and a choral reading that expresses the ancient need of peoples to express together the feelings that they share. Choric drama is rooted in primitive rituals and early Greek drama.

Initially, the Parkland Players were cool to the idea of presenting a play celebrating patriotism. "The story of our nation just hasn't been overwhelmingly appealing to students for quite some time," I told a reporter. "They are just not the sentimentalists of generations past."

Moreover, the month before the *Banner* project became a possibility, my Parkland students had seen another choric drama on a similar theme and were bored silly by it.

I had to do a little arm-twisting, persuading them in a short speech about how fortunate we are to be Americans. I also had them immerse themselves in the script, which they eventually found appealing.

Dr. Welch visited rehearsals and described herself as "on cloud nine" by what she saw. She called me "an absolutely brilliant director" and she said that my students had "tackled a most difficult art form in a most magnificent way." I had selected risers on which my students would perform and had given them solo, duo and trio parts to recite. The whole choric group responded to the most dominant messages of pride for our flag.

We presented *That Banner in the Sky* at the AAUW gathering, several times at Parkland and at drama festivals in Gastonia and Raleigh. By this time, it was April of 1976, and word of the production's success was getting around.

70

Those who saw the show, including School Superintendent C.C. Lipscombe of the N.C. Department of Public Instruction, felt it deserved national recognition. They recommended that the John F. Kennedy Center for the Performing Arts include it their presentations marking the Bicentennial. Rep. Stephen Neal (D), who represented North Carolina's Fifth District from 1975 to 1995, began looking at ways he could help bring the show to Washington as well.

In May of 1976, the Kennedy Center invited the Parkland Players to perform twice on Flag Day (June 14) at its Chautauqua Tent. In *The Nation's Stage: The John F. Kennedy Center for the Performing Arts*, Michael Dolan writes that the center's terrace-level atrium housed the tent, which aimed to recall summer programs of theater, music and lectures that started in Upstate New York in 1874 and spread nationwide until the 1920s. Between 1975 and 1976, the tent presented a series called "America on Stage," which showcased performances by community and school theaters from across the country. The Parkland Players' performance of *That Banner in the Sky* was a part of that series.

We ended up performing not only at the Chautauqua Tent but also on the steps of Lincoln and Jefferson Memorials. Thanks to Congressman Neal, several members of Congress saw us perform. The Chautauqua Tent performances drew

71

approximately 200 people. What a Bicentennial experience for me and my students!

Contributions to Non-Parkland Shows Whenever possible, the Parkland Players increased their experience by participating in non-Parkland shows.

In 1971, for example, they acted in a show I directed for Theater of the Word, an interdenominational group that performed Christian dramas. Dr. Joseph N. Patterson of Winston-Salem State University served as the show's narrator.

In August 1973, several Parkland Players made up the technical crew for my Freedom Street Players' performance of *Titusville*, a musical I wrote. The production, sponsored by the Urban Arts arm of the Arts Council of Winston-Salem and Forsyth County, was staged in several Winston-Salem venues, including the Governor's School-East of North Carolina, where I taught summer courses.

ACT IX

Teaching Career at the Career Center

WHEN THE WINSTON-SALEM/FORSYTH COUNTY Schools system opens its Career Center, in 1976, I am selected to teach its first Advanced Placement (AP) English class on a part-time basis. This means that for the next four years, I travel back and forth each day between the center and Parkland, teaching English mornings at the center and leading Parkland's drama program in the afternoons. In 1980, I am appointed to teach AP English full-time at the Career Center.

During a four-year period, I work at both the center and Parkland, some of my AP English students express an interest in participating in Parkland's productions, which means that they would rehearse at Parkland in the afternoons. I am happy to have these students participate--as long as I get their parents' consent and they keep up with their required readings of Dostoevsky, Tolstoy and Ibsen for AP English.

The involvement of the center's AP English students in Parkland's drama program would prove to be quite fruitful. One AP student writes *Adam and Eve*, a fine piece of experimental theater that I direct for the High School Play Festival of the North Carolina Theatre Conference. The Parkland Players create all the dance movements for *Adam and Eve*. All involved love working on this experimental piece, which receives the conference's highest honor.

The Career Center/Parkland collaborations would culminate in 1980 with a production of *Godspell*, a popular musical. Hilton Smith, one of my AP students, plays Lamar (Da Vinci) and serves as the production's chief guitarist. Ron Andrews, a Mars Hill College senior who becomes my student teacher at Parkland, serves as the choreographer and also plays Stephen (Jesus). (Mars Hill, near Asheville, is now named Mars Hill University.)

Ironically, in 1975, the Parkland Players create *The Goldfinders*, a musical that is thematically quite similar to *Godspell*. In *Goldfinders*, Simon (Jesus) has been followed to a mountaintop by a group of disillusioned young people. Their values are worse than those of the people they leave behind, and their greed causes them to crucify Simon, the show's protagonist. Luke, the antagonist of *Goldfinders*, later becomes Simon's Judge; Luke is played by Jihmi Kennedy, who later stars in *Glory*, a blockbuster movie.

In the spring of 1980, I step down as the director of the drama program at Parkland, having begun teaching AP English full-time at the Career Center. The Parkland Players are hardly finished with me, though. Many want to keep participating in shows I direct. So I begin the Flonnie Anderson Theatrical Association (FATA) to keep them doing just that. I conclude that the time for FATA is right, since I am no longer teaching drama classes and feel free to take my drama energies more into the Winston-Salem community.

It takes several months for FATA to stage Fred Ballard's *Ladies of the Jury*, its first show, and my former Parkland Players keep twisting my arm to get started. Another one of FATA's first productions, in the fall of 1981, is *The Death and Life of Sneaky Fitch*, a fable of the Olde West. The plan thereafter is to produce four shows a year, two of them original.

FATA presents another show in 1981: *Back to Creation*, having already staged *Creation* in 1977, casting Parkland and Career Center students. Rick Canter (one of my former students) runs sound for that production and performs in the one that FATA presents. In a *Sentinel* preview of FATA's *Creation*, Canter points out that half the 10-member cast are former Parkland students.

"The show deals with man being born into this world, but finds himself where he wants to make his own world instead of being where God wants him," Canter told *The Sentinel*. "Chaos results until man decides to go back to the Deity."

The *Sentinel* preview of FATA's *Creation* also states that a "new company, FATA, will present an original show that won awards four years ago for the Parkland Players. Flonnie Anderson's troupe brings back *Back to the Creation* at 7 p.m. tomorrow, Friday and Saturday at Wentz Memorial United Church of Christ."

Perhaps, the writer of the *Sentinel* preview does not know FATA is a new name for my Community Players Guild, organized in 1952. In any event, FATA would become a fixture in Winston-Salem for the next 34 years.

It takes some time for FATA to find a permanent home. Until the company does, it has access to several venues, including Wentz Memorial United Church of Christ, the Salem Fine Arts Center Workshop Theater and the Winston Square downtown (formerly Sawtooth Auditorium).

We do a variety of shows. One, Arthur Kopit's play *Chamber Music*, revolves around several women in an asylum who think they are famous women from various periods in history (e.g., Joan of Arc, Amelia Earhart and Constanze Mozart, the wife of the famous composer); the women are planning for an attack they believe is coming from the asylum's male ward. *Chamber Music* is hilarious! Our playbill also includes original mimes: The Movers and Toyshop. Mechanics and Farmers Bank, along with the Arts Council of Winston-Salem and Forsyth County, handles the ticket sales.

As time goes on through the 1980s, my schedule teaching AP English at the Career Center becomes quite heavy. When that happens, I lighten the load by accepting help from guest directors. Even with the extra help, I still direct at least one show a season. In 1982, I direct *South Pacific*. The following year I direct *Purlie*, a musical adapted from Ossie Davis' play, which was originally written for a predominantly black cast. Riley Matthews, a white music teacher from Parkland, plays one of the lead roles.

In 1983, I also direct a FATA production of *Medea*, the famed Greek tragedy. Half the show's cast consist of white Parkland graduates who'd since become very active FATA loyalists. Drama faculty at UNC School of the Arts see this show. They are so impressed that they invite my daughter Deirdre Anderson, who plays the title role, to enroll in UNCSA's School of Drama. She does. Two other cast members enroll along with her.

In 1984, I direct *Les Blanc* for FATA, casting multiple white actors who are better known for their work with the Little Theatre of Winston-Salem. The play deals with three African brothers as they face their own values regarding an impending revolution. *The Chronicle* newspaper of Winston-Salem writes, "This powerful drama of the rising tide of native rebellion and European military might bring a different sort of theater to Winston-Salem--very poignant and exciting."

Indeed, rebellion in a British-ruled African country reaches the height of art in the acting skills of Charlotte Blount as Dr. Goterling, Ken Conners as Dr. DeKoven, Roger Richardson as Major Rice, Jim Austin as a Yankee reporter and Robin Voiers as Madame Neilsen. Also excellent are the African brothers: Rudy Anderson Jr. plays Thshembe Matoseh; Bruce Foriest, Brother #2; and Toney Sealey, Brother #3.

Other shows I direct for FATA in 1980s include *A Raisin in the Sun*, *Bus Stop*, *Witness for the Prosecution* and *Deep are the Roots*.

In a "Tarheel Sketch" in the *Winston-Salem Journal*, Genie Carr reports me as saying: "It has become hard to juggle the teaching and the play rehearsals, the board meetings and all of that."

So, yes, I chose to retire from those memorable years at Atkins, Anderson, Parkland and the Career Center. But Carr also writes that "one kind of curtain is falling for Mrs. Anderson, although nobody believes that she will stay in the wings for long. She tried to exit without encores but the Career Center people had other ideas: a farewell bash was held at the Sawtooth Building. Its title: The Career Center Presents Flonnie Anderson."

Flonnie Anderson

INTERLUDE

My "Sistah" Encounters with Maya Angelou

IN 1982, SHORTLY AFTER MAYA ANGELOU BECAME the Reynolds Professor of American Studies at Wake Forest University, I received a call from Maya's close friend, Dr. Dolly McPherson, an English professor who became the first black woman to teach full time at the university. Dr. McPherson was inviting my husband and me to a get-acquainted dinner at Maya's first Winston-Salem home, on Valley Road.

I was very excited. Maya's poetry and prose, including the immensely popular *I Know Why The Caged Bird Sings*, the first installment in her six-part autobiography, had solidified her reputation as one of the leading lights of American literature. Her books were on the list of required readings for my AP English students at the Career Center. Now, I was going to meet this extremely talented and inspiring woman in the flesh. How was I to act? What was I to say to her? What did I say to her? I don't even remember.

What I do remember is that when Maya opened her own door, a statuesque queen of the literary universe extended her powerful hand to welcome her guests. She was a gracious entertainer and a dynamite cook. Her spaghetti and meatballs were scrumptious!

After our first meeting, I became "sistah" to her and she was indeed "sistah" to me. When my third son, Raymond Luron, died in 1991, Maya sent me and Rudy Sr. the most beautiful Calla Lillies.

I would socialize with Maya many times. For example, Rudy Sr., Deirdre and I were invited to many of Maya's birthday parties, the most elegant of which were hosted by Oprah Winfrey at the Grayland Estates. Our friends, the Ervins, Rudy Sr. and I decided that we needed limousine service for that. We even had a joyous time at an Oprah birthday party that took place at the High Point home of the parents of Stedman Graham, Oprah's lifetime partner.

In the 1990s, just before a housewarming party that took place in Maya's second Winston-Salem home, on Bartram Road, Oprah insisted that Rudy drive her from Valley Road to Maya's new home, not the driver of the limo originally hired to bring her and her secretary. Oprah sat up front with Rudy in my own Cadillac, and I sat in the car's backseat with Oprah's secretary. We had a big laugh about that.

I would ride in the backseat of my Cadillac many times after that because, as Rudy Sr. often said, "The front passenger seat is sacred. Oprah sat here."

My relationship with Maya soon evolved into a professional one. Maya and I spent many hours in her den revising her script for *Sister, Sister*, a television drama from 1982, to a staged performance by students at Wake Forest University. Maya had granted me permission to direct her play for Wake Forest's drama department. This project came about because Dr. Harold Tedford, then the director of Wake Forest University Theatre, had asked me to direct a play of my choice that would attract participation of minority students.

After working with Maya on the script, we both marveled at the results. *Sister, Sister* the television drama became *Sisters* the play. It featured a phenomenal cast and drew a packed house at Ring Theatre on Wake Forest's campus.

My WFU collaboration with Maya would be the first of many. For example, when I directed Barefoot, an opera performed at

83

Flonnie Anderson

Winston-Salem State University's Kenneth R. Williams Auditorium, I cast students from the Best Choice Center in the chorus of singing voices, and, when I called on Maya to narrate, she graciously consented. The production created quite a buzz.

Maya's "sistah" encounters with me increased after *Barefoot*. I enjoyed a number of afternoon snacks with Maya at her home on Valley Road. Then came the opportunity to be cast in the first performance of her two-character play *On A Southern Journey*, which was directed by Pat Toole, an instructor in the speech and theatre department at Wake Forest University. As the *Winston-Salem Journal* reported on July 18, 1983, the production's other actress was Diane Rousseau, a popular soap opera star. The play premiered at the Scales Fine Arts Center at WFU; for me, this was a stellar experience as an actress.

I was so motivated by Maya's interest in my skills at the time that when I was asked to read Black poetry for a program at Reynolda House Museum of American Art, in Winston-Salem, I selected one of Maya's latest poems to include on the program. This was "On the Pulse of Morning," which Maya wrote for and recited at the first inauguration of President Bill Clinton, in 1993.

After my program at Reynolda House was over, several of Maya's students who were present thanked me for giving them a better understanding of the meaning of "On the Pulse of the

84

Morning," crediting my vocal interpretation. It is a powerful piece of poetry.

I conclude my memories of Maya with an appreciation for her support of FATA. She hosted some of the company's business meetings at her home on Valley Road, and these were very special.

Of course, I held some business meetings at my home, on Kinard Drive. When meetings took place at my home, Maya was invariably absent and Dr. McPherson always seemed to have a nice excuse for Maya's inability to attend.

You see, Dr. McPherson made decisions regarding Maya's meanders in Winston-Salem. Perhaps, she felt it necessary to limit Maya's trips to "the hood." Of course, I could always call Maya's private number when I needed to talk to her.

Anytime my sisters would encounter Maya at Mt. Zion Baptist Church, where Maya and my sisters worshipped, Maya would tell them, "Tell Flonnie I love her."

Even now, several years after Maya's death, I cannot think of her as gone.

Flonnie Anderson

ACT X

Retirement?
Flonnie's Just Getting Started in the 1990s

WHAT DO I REALLY WANT TO DO after retiring from the Winston-Salem/Forsyth County Schools? Several answers emerge.

One answer, namely satisfying my passion for creating a one-woman show that reflects historical reality, becomes dominant. So, I dramatize "The Quarters," the last section of *The Autobiography of Miss Jane Pittman*, the 1971 novel by Ernest J. Gaines. I become fascinated by the storyline, and I love the language, which brings back memories of my childhood, my own grandparents, my aunt, my mother and my father.

My experiences performing *The Quarters* would make me very happy. I present the show for a Sigma Gamma Rho sorority and at such venues as Reynolda House Museum of American Art, the Hickory Museum of Art, and the Marriott in Charlotte (for a national convention of National Women of Achievement Inc.) I also do the show for a "First Night" program of the Arts Council of Winston-Salem and Forsyth County.

For me, *The Quarters* is like a dream come true, and in the 1990s, I also perform the show in addition to "Strolling Clowns and Mime" at the Corpening Plaza for a "Carolina Street Scene" presentation by the Arts Council of Winston-Salem and Forsyth County.

Critiques of *The Quarters* appear several times in various publications. One of the reviews really inflates my ego; this is the one that Julie Boutwell wrote for *Old Gold and Black*, the Wake Forest University newspaper at which she served as the arts and entertainment editor. In the March 30, 1990, edition of *Gold and Black*, Boutwell writes:

"Although the entire play was a monologue, Anderson captured Jane's story so realistically that audience members felt they knew 'The Quarters' as well as Jane. They felt they could see the rows of shackled houses along the street and the many acres of corn blowing in the wind. They knew Jimmy [the protagonist] as a sensitive child and a virtuous adult...They could also feel the rage over Jimmy's untimely death, the dark figures marching toward the courthouse and Jane slowly walking in the front with her wooden cane."

Critic Genie Carr also praises my *Quarters* show. "It's a story whose telling requires the balancing of gravity and a gentle wry wit," Carr writes in the *Winston-Salem Journal*. "Mrs. Anderson brings those characteristics to Jane Pittman. Her movement and the very brief moments of mental drifting--eyes closed, head against the back of the rocking chair--had just enough to remind us of the age of the lady without distracting us from her graceful telling of a powerful story."

During the 1990s, the *Quarters* show is just one of many projects and activities keeping me very busy. In 1991, for example, I prepare *They Do Come Home*, an original full-length play, to present at the first annual North Carolina Playwrights Festival, which is hosted by University of North Carolina at Greensboro.

At the request of Dr. McPherson, I submit commentary to the *New York Times* in response to an op-ed that Maya Angelou published on Clarence Thomas in that paper on Sunday, Aug. 25, 1991.

My Whirlwind

I organize a FATA-sponsored pop/rap showcase that is presented in the Kenneth R. Williams Auditorium at Winston-Salem State University.

The Drama and Speech Department at Wake Forest University hires me to guest-direct a production of Maya Angelou's *Sisters* in its Ring Theater.

Between 1992 and 1995, I become particularly busy. You can find me on the campus of Salem College shooting scenes for a film called *Taking Liberty*. I also accept awards for my work in community theater, play bridge to relax, and participate in "Shorts for Lunch," readings of literature sponsored by N.C. School of the Arts (now UNC School of the Arts). I star in "African-American Poetry with Flonnie Anderson," a program at Reynolda House Museum of American Art.

In 1995, FATA produces *J.B.* (1958), Archibald MacLeish's free verse adaptation of the biblical story of Job. The show becomes a smash hit, prompting Dorothy Bigby, the editor of the *Wentz Witness*, the newsletter for Wentz Memorial United Church of Christ, to write the following words in that publication:

"Well, Flonnie, you did it again! You took something that seemed impossible and made it outstanding, inspirational and personally challenging to every on-looker and volunteer for this presentation. Your insight and dramatic expertise taught many the true story of Job, what he endured, how he handled temptation, ridicule and utter destruction, as well as reminding Biblical scholars, readers, teachers and ministers that there is always something else to learn about what you thought you already knew."

After *J.B.*, FATA, Old Salem and SECCA collaborate on a show called "The Spirit of Fred Wilson: Remembering Old Salem." This is part of "Memory," an exhibit designed to reexamine Old Salem's past role and its present place in history. I write the script and direct presentations of the show, which takes place on the grounds adjacent to Home Moravian Church. If I remember correctly, FATA performs "Memory" 36 times for 3000 tourists.

Mel White, SECCA's project director, sends me a wonderful letter of thanks following "The Spirit of Fred Wilson."

"Please accept our congratulations on an outstanding performance by FATA," White wrote. "Everyone seemed to have loved this new interpretation of Part I of 'Memory.' Even with the rain, the attendance reflected a high interest in FATA's role in the exhibit."

Susan Lubowsky, then SECCA's executive director, also wrote me a nice thank you letter.

"I just wanted to take this opportunity to thank you and the troupe for your spectacular success in re-envisioning Fred Wilson's project," reads Lubowsky's letter. "Each time I saw the performances they got better and better. Others felt the same--all the feedback from visitors and from the schools has been overwhelmingly enthusiastic. You all really made it happen. We are grateful to each of you."

In the mid-1990s, I suddenly realize that I have far too many projects on my plate. I need to slow down, so I decide to take on something fun but less intense. I participate in fashion shows and judge Shakespeare oratorical contests with Pat Toole and Eric Kirshner, two instructors in speech and drama at Wake Forest University.

I write and direct *Dem Dry Bonz*, a play based on scripture, for a program at Wentz United Memorial Church of Christ. I graciously accept a *Winston-Salem Chronicle* Cultural Arts Award.

When I assess my whirlwind life again, in early 1998, I am rehearsing the lead chorus role in a Collective Theatre Company production of *Murder in the Cathedral* by T.S. Eliot. The show, directed by Eric Kerchner, is staged at Goler Metropolitan AME Zion Church and Wait Chapel of Wake Forest University.

Kerchner would later become the executive director of the Children's Museum of Winston-Salem. (A flier attached to Goler's and Wait's doors during the show reads: "Boycott Murder in the Cathedral.")

Murder receives rave reviews. Roger Moore, in his review for the *Winston-Salem Journal*, wrote: "Nothing short of the theatrical event of the year is happening at Goler Metropolitan AME Zion Church through Saturday night. The happy confluence of subject, setting and staging makes the Collective Theatre's production of T.S. Eliot's *Murder in the Cathedral* one of those shows that absolutely should not be missed."

James Dodding, a native of London, directed plays each spring at Wake Forest University from 1979 through 1998, when he retired. "I was privileged to be in your audience last evening for *Murder in the Cathedral*," Dodding wrote me after seeing the show. "I want to thank you for the detailed, moving and exquisite performance. I know the play well, having directed it in a cathedral in England. You brought out the play's beauty and meaning so memorably. Thank you for uplifting my spirit."

In 1999, Rudy and I celebrate our 50th wedding anniversary. *The Chronicle* of Winston-Salem presents me a Lifetime Achievement Award.

Flonnie Anderson

ACT XI

2000 and Beyond

SINCE 1982, I HAVE BEEN A MEMBER of the Winston-Salem chapter of National Women of Achievement, Inc. (NWOA). I also serve as the organization's national recording secretary for four years, attending meetings in Houston and Fort Worth at least three times a year. Although my increasing involvement with FATA often limits my affiliation with the Winston-Salem chapter, I remain a loyal supporter of NWOA.

Beginning in 2000, several shows are added to FATA's repertoire. Among them are *Let My People Go* (in 2000); *Soul Gone Home* (2002); and *Sculpted Freedom* (2004), which is about Peter Oliver, a late-18th Century African-American craftsman whose descendant enlists my help in writing the show's script and directing the production. Dr. Raymond Oliver, the descendent and a skilled dentist, is very pleased with the production.

In 2004, I am the narrator of *Barefoot*, an opera staged by the Arts Based Elementary School in Winston-Salem. I create *Rise, Carver, Rise*, a back-to-school salute to Carver Senior High School in my community. I receive Wentz UCC's Author & Playwright Award.

In 2007, I create *Remus*, a now-famous musical fable adapted from Joel Chandler Harris' *Tales of Uncle Remus.* I write the script as well as the lyrics to all the songs. Remus becomes a hit for FATA, running for five seasons.

In 2008, reporting on an Anderson Senior High School class reunion, a reporter for the *Winston-Salem Chronicle* writes that "Mrs. Anderson taught her students how to make their writing an extension of themselves and encouraged them to participate in plays." Perhaps, I thought, *Remus* demonstrates that I am at the height of what I have advised my students to do. In any event, the show was arguably a crown achievement. It gives me such joy to produce it. Awards come in from the Pffaftown chapter of NWOA, the YMCA, the *Chronicle*, and Wentz. My Easter program is also quite successful.

In 2009, FATA repeated *J.B.* and *Remus*. The following year, FATA staged *Still Freed from the Sting of Death*, which was written by Larretta Rivera-Williams, a FATA sister. Rudy Sr. and I celebrated our 61st wedding anniversary. That milestone prompted me to say: "Bravo!" because our children hired a jazz band to help us celebrate. Jazz is Rudy Sr.'s favorite music.

Although Becky Brown, a fellow AP English teacher who became one of my revered friends, could not attend the celebration of our wedding anniversary, she penned "Flonnie Thoughts," some prose in my honor. The opening paragraph:

"I'd hear it in the hall: 'I've been slashed! She slashed me again!' I would know that Flonnie had been grading essays. Students have the talent of filling pages with fluff--using lots of words and saying absolutely nothing. Flonnie would have none of it. Whole paragraphs would get her big slash. She taught many students to be better writers and, more importantly, she made them aware that vacuous thought and lazy logic would be discovered and exposed! Her appreciation for the genuine and her disdain for superficiality are what drew me to Flonnie from the beginning."

Becky really helped me to realized who I am. I thought that I just didn't appreciate a lot of crap.

In 2011, I direct *A Woman Called Truth* for Stained Glass Playhouse of Winston-Salem. The following year, I direct the same play for FATA--and play the Sojourner, the lead role, not because I intend to but because the lead disappears 1 ½ weeks before opening night.

By 2014, I am pretty worn out. But that does not thwart my fascination with Pam Rea's play *Angels without Wings*. In 2015, I direct the show, a kind of two-act ministry about addiction. That's a serious subject, but a clever staging lends itself to high-quality theater.

I have begun to slow down quite a bit, but on October 7-9, 2016, I present for my church's 95th anniversary celebration my one-woman play: *The Quarters*, adapted from *The Autobiography of Miss Jane Pittman*.

EPILOGUE

On March 5, 2016, the Parkland Magnet High School Auditorium was dedicated in honor of Flonnie Anderson.

My family was present. Also in attendance were city representatives, including Mayor Allen Joines, school board representative Darrell Walker, and representatives of each of the four high schools where Anderson had taught them.

In March 2018, at a celebration in Winston Square Park, I was named one of four Distinguished Women in the Arts in Winston-Salem. The three other honorees were actress Rosemary Harris, poet Nell Davis Britton, and the late sculptor Earline King. Joines gave me a plaque, which I placed on a wall in my home, and a monument honoring me and the other distinguished women was erected in the park.

I am deeply humbled. Please remember that one person can be God's beam of light for hundreds of young people. Never underestimate what growth can be like when one is dedicated to the education of young people. TEACHING IS THE MOST NOBLE PROFESSION. Follow your passion! Your life will be rewarding! If it isn't, you have chosen the wrong path.

I close this memoir by sharing a few other reflections on my life. See appendix.

APPENDIX 1

"To Our Mother, A Fearsome Force of Nature"
By sons Rudy Jr. and Roscoe Mica

"She does not play when it comes to education or the arts."

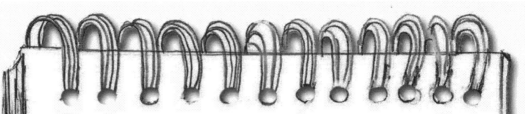

For those who know her, Flonnie T. Anderson has always been a fearsome force of nature. She does not play when it comes to education or the arts. Educated in the Winston-Salem/Forsyth County Schools (actually the segregated Winston-Salem school system of the 1930s and 1940s), she dreamed of being a star on stage and on the big screen, when most occupations for African American women of the time were mostly relegated to education, domestic work, or working in the factory.

She left Winston-Salem to attend West Virginia State College. She told her parents she intended to pursue a degree in education with a concentration in English and French. But, when it came time for her to declare her major, her passion took over. It would be drama – and for hundreds of her students, they are glad she did.

She taught, oh yes, but along the way, she decided she wanted to establish an outlet that would showcase theatrical talent in the African American community. She established the Community Players Guild in the early 1950s, the first black community theatre in the South.

She branched out in 1956, playing the role of Tituba in Arthur Miller's *The Crucible* at the Winston-Salem Little Theatre, making her the first African American actor in the theatre's history.

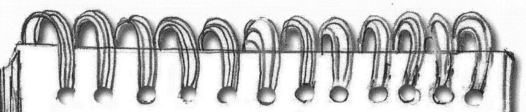

"She told me I had talent and that she would share with me everything she had," recalled Jihmi Kennedy, a 1975 graduate of Parkland High School. "It was the first time I felt aware of something I hadn't known I had. She taught me the fundamentals of the craft." She inspired many others, not only in the schools but in the wider community as well.

Her community productions included such notable works as Ossie Davis' *Purlie Victorious*, Rodgers & Hammerstein's *Oklahoma*! and South Pacific, Lorraine Hansberry's *A Raisin in the Sun* and many others. She continued to be a vibrant force in live theater with her own company, the Flonnie Anderson Theatrical Association (FATA).

She has performed her one-woman show adapted from *The Autobiography of Miss Jane Pittman* at the Reynolds House of American Art in Winston-Salem and other venues, and she herself portrayed Sojourner Truth in the PBS Bicentennial special.

It is for these reasons, and others too numerous to mention, that we respectfully honor mother in this memoir for her many cultural and educational contributions to this community.

Sons Rudy Jr. and Roscoe Mica

APPENDIX 2

Mother Mother Mother
By daughter Deirdre Anderson in 1993

Mother Mother Mother

I stood at the edge of the yard, my left hand held lightly by a smooth, but firm grip of a right hand. For some reason, we had stopped walking, and mother had turned me gently, but firmly to face her, her left hand squeezing my right shoulder, alternating with little patting motions. My mother has always been a demonstration.

When she knew that she had my full attention, she lifted her left pat from my shoulder and pointed her finger straight down at the edge of the yard where we were standing.

"This is the edge of your yard," she emphasized "your."

Mother, then pointed to the long, fascinating stretch of round beyond the yard's edge. As I turned to look at the road, she gently, but firmly turned my face to meet her eyes. Whenever my mother does this, nobody dares look any place else except her eyes.

"Never stop from the edge of your yard before you have looked lone and hard up the road and down the road, & up the road and down the road to be sure that no cars are coming," she said as she turned my face to survey the long length of road, my eyes peering far up the road and then far down the road before she turned me to look into her eyes once again for a repeat of her demonstration.

Thorough and protective. That is my mother, but she is also gentle and firm, injecting a bit of her actress background each time she speaks.

She almost always uses her hands in a rhythmic fashion. She can mesmerize whole groups of people, those hands and eyes.

At 315 West Twenty-Fifth Street where I grew up, even when she used to rock me back and forth on her lap, her song was low and mellow, and her eyes always seemed to smile then. A lot of times, I would doze off to sleep looking at her content eyes and feeling those soothing hands caress me.

When I crushed my right elbow, the doctor told my mother that I would never use my right arm effectively again. She did not believe the doctor and proceeded to involve me in a series of her own rehabilitative exercises. I later became the best basketball, softball and volleyball player in junior high. Her determination is awesome.

My mother is also a very positive person. Even when everyone else believers that something cannot happen, she believes that it can and sets out to prove the impossible possible. Many times, in getting the task done, she may be stern, authoritative, and seemingly inconsiderate, but she is also exciting, energetic, and hard working. When she taught students who were not expected to achieve, she was relentless in preparing them to prove their detractors wrong.

In preparing her students for a Wake Forest Speech Festival in 1954, where no group of color had ever competed before, she made them practice seven days per week, only having lunch and dinner breaks and eight hours of sleep at night. She instilled the power of determination in them and boosted their self-confidence and pride in achievement, sometimes not without tears. The students took every superior rating at the festival and won the Sweepstake Award to everybody's amazement, except my mother's.

She is an original in style and grace.

She still glides as she walks with her imitable artistic flare. Her kind of theatre is very interesting, illuminating and always inspiring. "Versatile," is perhaps one of the best words to describe my mother. She plays bridge too and wins all the time.

Written by daughter Deirdre Anderson in 1993

APPENDIX 3

A Life Experience

Entry Written for
An English Assignment
By Cindy Letchworth.

"Take Me Higher"

PARKLAND HIGH SCHOOL

Take Me
Higher

Take Me
Higher

Take Me
Higher

Take Me Higher

My senior year began in August, 1970 at Parkland High School in Winston Salem, North Carolina. I had looked forward to this year since I began as a "Mighty Mustang" sophomore. I had already completed most of the classes required for college admission, so no more math this year. My schedule included the challenging classes of English, European History, and Chemistry, but now there was room in my schedule to take Drama, Current Events, and Typing.

As seniors, my classmates and I had the privilege of leaving campus each day for lunch. I danced on the drill team, the Dixie Debs, and participated in many clubs. It would be fun to spend more time with friends whom I rarely saw during the summer.

However, my classmates and I faced a huge change this year. In an effort to desegregate the public schools, the Winston-Salem/Forsyth County Schools administration decided to close Atkins, an all-black high school, and reassign all of its students to Parkland. Many of its teachers would also be transferred. In my first two years, a small number of black students had attended Parkland through the system's "freedom of choice policy." Now for the Atkins students, there wouldn't' be a choice.

I'd like to say that everyone was pleased with the decision and all of us were looking forward to sharing new friendships and experiences. But minimally, people were concerned, and many, afraid. And truthfully, some were outright disgusted. We'd heard stories from other schools in other places of fights and violence in the midst of this forced integration.

I wondered how it would feel to have attended Atkins for several years and then be ordered to change schools. What would happen with school clubs and teams and class rank? At that stage in my life I did feel concerns for my future classmates, but it didn't even occur to me to wonder how those teachers must have felt, to have had to change their place of employment and their position in the pecking order of the faculty at a different school.

That year, and in the next few years to follow, private white church-sponsored schools emerged like mushrooms after a big rain. These schools enforced strict policies about who could attend, the attire and length of hair of those students, and the morality (or lack thereof) of their chosen curriculum.

The school year began fairly smoothly, in spite of the tension in the atmosphere. No doubt there must have been quarrels and fights, but nothing so severe that we all had something to talk about. On the other hand, we students still continued to segregate ourselves in our social circles and in classrooms without assigned seats.

Mrs. Flonnie Anderson, a drama teacher from Anderson High, became my favorite teacher that year. Charged with electronic energy, she turned us on to acting, reading a

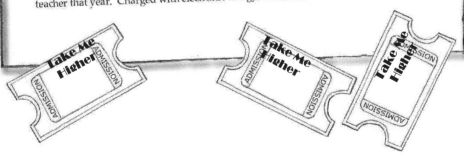

variety of plays, and creating stage sets. Her bright brown eyes, like polished smoky quartz, sparkled, and her fly-away Afro hairstyle reminded me of science experiments that taught the effects of static electricity. With her as our teacher, drama didn't turn out to be the easy class I had expected. She put her heart into her work and expected the same from us. She took us out of our comfort zones, but she inspired us to be creative. She required us to read much, use stage lighting effectively, and memorize many lines.

Mrs. Anderson's teen-age son, along with some other students, wrote a play entitled Take Me Higher. This drama was not a typical story, but a statement. The young playwrights believed that pointing out many of our nation's problems at the time, such as racism, the "generation gap," and the Viet Nam War, would help us solve these problems. Mrs. Anderson assigned each of us in the drama classes a role. At the beginning, a white male student portrayed the United States of America, standing tall and proud, much like the Statue of Liberty. As the scenes revealed more and more of the problems of those times, he was replaced by a black female student, wearing a leotard and tights, who moved in a slow, fluid dance, bending and falling. I danced a minuet in the first act of the play, my only part, but I loved watching my classmates with larger roles speaking, acting, and dancing until the end. The theme song was "I Want to Take You Higher," a popular tune recorded by Sly and the Family Stone. Our well-integrated cast rehearsed often, began performing for audiences in November, and became friends along the way.

Mrs. Anderson made arrangements with our principal and school staff to give the performance several evenings, mostly for our parents, but we also scheduled it for our student body to see during their study skills class periods. The first show made us proud, with the thunder of applause at the end.

S o it came as a shock, we were totally alarmed and dismayed, when a man in the audience stood up and started shouting during one of our daytime performances. "You sinners," he screamed. "This play was written by Satan!" He continued to yell as our assistant principal escorted him out of the auditorium. We struggled to recover and finish the play that day, but we felt as if we'd been unplugged from the source of all our energy.

Later that evening, the man appeared on local television news, stating that our play condoned nudity, drugs, and immorality.

He told TV viewers that out leotard-clad leading lady stood on stage naked. Who was this guy? Perhaps he was a member of the John Birch Society. I don't remember his name of what church he represented, but his accusations started an uproar in our community. Sadly, many folks believed him, because they never saw the play. Letters to the editor protesting our production appeared in the Winston-Salem Journal, many referring to Mrs. Anderson and her son as evil.

While the accusations flew outside our school, inside we connected. We grew closer and supported each other. Even students not enrolled in drama classes stood on our side. As a united front, we defended Mrs. Anderson, our play, and its playwrights. We protested when instructed to suspend performances. Our efforts didn't change things right away, but they brought us together, college-bound and general curriculum students, sophomores to seniors, black and whites. Mrs. Anderson continued teaching, coaching us in our classes with enthusiasm and spunk. She kept her head up and her standards high. Eventually, we did perform Take Me Higher again, after the controversy had lost its spark, and our parents and the artistic members of our city had had their say. Our cast took the play on the road to a festival in Raleigh toward the end of the school year.

During those first years of de-segregation, some schools have had stories about how sports teams helped them unite and work together. Playing together on athletic teams did help students get along at Parkland High School. But what brought us together and helped us overcome many of our differences most of all was that stormy play with its rock'n'roll theme song, Take Me Higher, and its director, Mrs. Flonnie Anderson.

APPENDIX 4

My Teacher, My Mentor, My Friend
By Teresa D. Hairston

(years after being a high school drama student at Parkland)

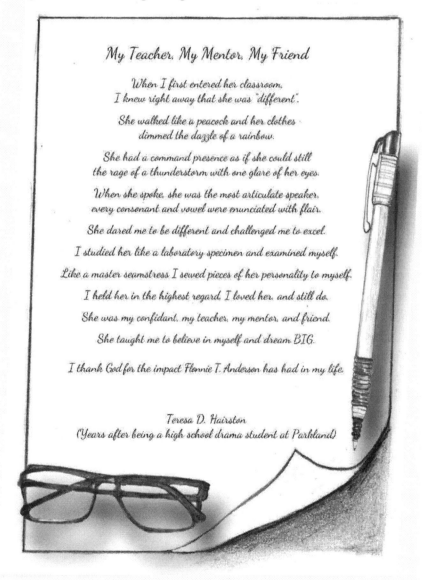

My Teacher, My Mentor, My Friend

When I first entered her classroom,
I knew right away that she was "different".

She walked like a peacock and her clothes
dimmed the dazzle of a rainbow.

She had a command presence as if she could still
the rage of a thunderstorm with one glare of her eyes.

When she spoke, she was the most articulate speaker,
every consonant and vowel were enunciated with flair.

She dared me to be different and challenged me to excel.

I studied her like a laboratory specimen and examined myself.

Like a master seamstress I sewed pieces of her personality to myself.

I held her in the highest regard, I loved her, and still do.

She was my confidant, my teacher, my mentor, and friend.

She taught me to believe in myself and dream BIG.

I thank God for the impact Flonnie T. Anderson has had in my life.

Teresa D. Hairston
(Years after being a high school drama student at Parkland)

APPENDIX 5

Letter from Rudolph and Sarah Boone

3151 Butterfield Drive
Winston Salem, N.C. 27105

January 4, 2016

Mrs. Flonnie T. Anderson
550 Kinard Drive
Winston-Salem, N.C. 27101

Dear Mrs. Anderson,

Enclosed please find a check for $100.00. Please feel free to use it for whatever you choose!

This is a heartfelt expression of our love, respect and gratitude for your many years of faithful, dedicated service and outstanding contributions to educating numerous children and adults of this school district and beyond.

Congratulations on the auditorium at Parkland High School being named in your honor! This is a much deserved and lone overdue recognition!

We are happy for this opportunity to demonstrate, in a tangible way our appreciation for your many contributions and sacrifices. Your teaching and example have made positive impact on the lives of thousands of young people! Many of your students have become outstanding citizens, leaders, professionals, individuals and family people. They are making our society a better place for themselves and everyone else!

It was a pleasure and honor to have been one of your co-workers at Anderson Jr. Sr. High School! We all recognize your talents, skills, accomplishments, sacrifices and dedication then, and now we are happy to know that others are doing the same. My God continue to bless you with honors and recognition that you so richly deserve.

Sincerely,

Rudolph V. Sr. and Sarah

Rudolph V. Sr. and Sarah J. Boone

Date 01/04/2016

Anderson $ 100.00

APPENDIX 6

Letter From Ben Trawick

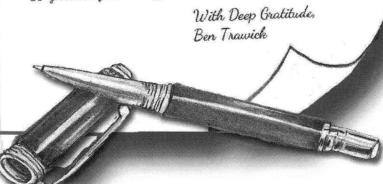

10/19/2016

Dear Mrs. Anderson,

I pause today to write a thank you note that is more than 30 years overdue. In 1980-81 I was a student in your AP grammar and composition class at the career center. In the way of 16 years old, I left your classroom at the end of the year without pausing to appreciate properly your love, labor and instruction.

When I recently came across the article about you having been honored by Parkland High School, it spurred me to express _____. I hold you in honor as well. You gave me two great gifts— first, you encouraged me as a writer and helped me to understand (perhaps as a result of your drama background) the importance of evocative writing. You were significant in giving me confidence as a writer. Secondly, you nominated me to attend the NC Governor School in English——a phenomenal privilege that I took for granted at the time. I now appreciate more fully that good teachers mark our lives in lasting ways.

Please receive, from a 52-year old, the thanks that a 16-year old failed to offer.

With Deep Gratitude,
Ben Trawick

.

APPENDIX 7

"From the Acknowledgements Page of a 2017
Work of Short Stories by Lu Ann Tucker"

Acknowledgements

My thanks, love and appreciation to God first for all of his blessings He has given me. Secondly, thanks to my parents Bertha C. Tucker and James E. Tucker, and my family for all of their love and support. Special thanks to Pastor Constance York and Mrs. Shelley Madison for critiquing my writing and being such a blessing in my life.

I think that everyone has a favorite teacher. For me, that teacher is Mrs. Flonnie T. Anderson. She taught English and Literature at Anderson High School in Winston Salem, North Carolina. I remember her kindness and interest in wanting all of her students to succeed in life. She encouraged me to write and was so instrumental in my life. She invested herself in my life and gave me hope. I'm honored to have been one of her students. I never stopped reading.

Thank you Mrs. Anderson.

To those in the body of Christ, who diligently pray for me, I dedicate this book and pray that it blesses you as much as I was blessed as I wrote it.

Finally, to all of you who will read this book share it. May it warm your hearts and prompt the gifts within you.

124

APPENDIX 8

To: My Sister
From: Jeanette T. Lewis

To My Sister

From Jeanette T. Lewis

I always call you the March Wind.
(You were born March 5th). Your March
winds blow in many directions.

You always motivate, energize
and influence so many young
people and the not so young.
For that and so much more, I
thank God for my sister.

APPENDIX 9

"To the Woman I Love and Most Admire!"

Made in the USA
Middletown, DE
18 November 2019